# 30 Minutes
## ... To Make the
## Right Impression

**Eleri Sampson**

**KOGAN
PAGE**

The right of Eleri Sampson to be identified as the author of this work has been asserted by her in accordance with the Copyright, Designs and Patents Act 1988.

**British Library Cataloguing in Publication Data**
A CIP record for this book is available from the British Library.
ISBN 0 7494 2525 3

Typeset by Florencetype Ltd, Stoodleigh, Devon
Printed and bound in Great Britain by Clays Ltd, St Ives plc

# CONTENTS

# The 30 Minutes Series

The *Kogan Page 30 Minutes Series* has been devised to give your confidence a boost when faced with tackling a new skill or challenge for the first time.

So the next time you're thrown in at the deep end and want to bring your skills up to scratch or pep up your career prospects, turn to the *30 Minutes Series* for help!

*Titles available are:*

30 Minutes Before Your Job Interview

30 Minutes Before a Meeting

30 Minutes Before a Presentation

30 Minutes to Boost Your Communication Skills

30 Minutes to Brainstorm Great Ideas

30 Minutes to Deal with Difficult People

30 Minutes to Succeed in Business Writing

30 Minutes to Master the Internet

30 Minutes to Make the Right Decision

30 Minutes to Make the Right Impression

30 Minutes to Plan a Project

30 Minutes to Prepare a Job Application

30 Minutes to Write a Business Plan

30 Minutes Write a Marketing Plan

30 Minutes to Write a Report

30 Minutes to Write Sales Letters

*Available from all good booksellers.*
*For further information on the series, please contact:*

Kogan Page, 120 Pentonville Road, London N1 9JN
Tel: 020 7278 0433 Fax: 020 7837 6348

**1**

# INTRODUCTION
# The psychology of
# first impressions

*Somewhere in time society lost the plot. We decided that how a person looked was more important than who that person was.*

Anita Roddick, *Full Voice*, 1996

## Introduction

If we lived in a different kind of world, people would judge us for our hard work, loyalty and effort. The reality is that people who work hard and keep their head down get overlooked: those with good personal PR get the rewards. If you package yourself appropriately you will get noticed and be appreciated more. If you look inefficient and badly organized, we think you must be an inefficient and badly organized person whether you are or not. Successful relationships in our business life and our social life depend on how we manage our behaviour in different situations with different people, creating an appropriate impression.

## First impressions

Research shows that we don't have 30 minutes to make the right impression. A strong impression is made within moments and a lasting opinion is based on how we look, sound and move within half a minute to four minutes. Few of us are free from irrational prejudice – men with beards, women in trousers, the Welsh, the Irish, etc. In our life, we all play many parts. Research shows that we have less than four minutes to make an impression on someone we meet for the first time. First impressions are made up of a two-way trans-action in which people send out and receive complex infor-mation about themselves – who they are and what they stand for. The initial impact is created by the way we look, the way we move and the way we sound as well as what we have to say. Our perception of strangers is dominated by what we see, so we focus on their dress, grooming, gestures and facial expression. Next we focus on what we can hear; things such as the tone of their voice, their accent and how loudly they speak. Finally, we focus on the words themselves.

*So far as other people are concerned you are your behaviour. Although there are other things which go towards making you the person you are – your thoughts, feelings, attitudes, motives, beliefs and so on – your behaviour is apparent to everyone.*

Dr Peter Honey, Psychologist and
Specialist in Interactive Skills

If you have got 30 minutes there are things you can do in terms of preparation, planning and research that will go a long way towards creating that right impression. We process this information in order to get ready to meet what we presume is going to be a certain kind of person. We try to interpret the signals against our own knowledge, experience and prejudice. We absorb, then edit the information we receive, sometimes for its own sake but usually for practical reasons. The material is used to help us to define the situation. We ask ourselves questions such as: 'Is this person potentially safe or dangerous?' 'What behaviour will be needed from me?' 'What kind of behaviour can I expect from the other person?'

We are led to believe that judgements are made within minutes. Indeed they are but some people take longer than others to sum up a stranger. Physical characteristics such as age, gender and ethnicity are conveyed visually and instantly via height, weight, colouring and facial features. Other characteristics such as intelligence, competence, confidence, social class, attractiveness, financial status and so on are then deduced – not always accurately. Some people have difficulty reading the non-verbal cues. Some of us use our intuition, others rely on the facts as they see them, weighing up the evidence before reaching a conclusion. This can take time, not just minutes but weeks or months. In many situations we don't know how much time it will take for other people to make judgements about us, so it's as well we try to make a good impression first time round.

## From the inside out

My approach to impression management is a holistic one. I don't believe you can separate the way you look and behave from the way you think and feel. Which is why I use an INSIDE>OUT approach. Your attitude, emotions and thinking work their way outwards and are displayed through your behaviour. You can't *not* make an impression. If you learn to control the messages you send out you can consciously project the image of yourself you intended to project. Successful relationships in business life depend on how we manage our behaviour in different situations with different people.

## Impression management

When people visit another country, go to their friends or stay with their family they automatically 'accommodate' to the people they are with. They modify their accent or speak more quickly maybe or just fall into the familiar family shorthand. When talking to a young child we make our vocabulary simpler: when communicating to a deaf person we articulate more clearly. This is all part of the human ability to handle language. A similar process is at work in terms of our behaviour when we meet people and want to make a good impression. Because we are not all innately skilled at accommodating our behaviour and appearance to other people when we want to create the right impression, it's useful to understand some of the psychological background and learn a few techniques.

There are nine stages in impression management.

1. Identify your goals – what do *you* want to get out of the situation?

2. Identify your audience.

3. Select the appropriate tools and techniques to achieve your goals.

4. Do the deed, demonstrate the behaviour.
5. Assess the audience's reaction.
6. Assess to what extent personal outcomes have been met.
7. Reshape or retain tools or techniques.
8. Reshape or retain personal goals.
9. Do it again.

## 'Putting on a show'

Putting on a show is perfectly natural behaviour because in our lives we all play many parts. We create social identities to fill social, personal or business needs. We are the same character all the time but we have to play different roles in our lifestyle – mother, daughter, friend, wife, colleague, boss, businessperson, professional presenter. Think of a recent example when it was important that you came over well. It might have been at a boring lecture where you wanted to impress the lecturer with your alertness and intellectual capacity. Maybe you were planning to visit your partner's family or maybe you had a job interview recently. Try to capture a flashback of your thoughts and feelings at the time and see how honestly you can answer the questions.

1. Did you change your behaviour and put on a show?
2. To what extent did you modify your behaviour?
3. Why did you think it was necessary?
4. How did you feel at the time?
5. How did you feel afterwards?
6. Would you do it again if you had to?
7. What would happen if you didn't do it?

9

## 'Slipping backstage'

Putting on a show or keeping up appearances, even for a good cause, can be exhausting if you have to sustain it for too long. So it's important to find an opportunity to drop the mask and to be yourself. If making small talk and being sociable to people you don't know (and possibly don't even like) doesn't come naturally, why not take time out now and again. There are always opportunities to 'slip backstage' at a wedding reception or company conference. Decide to limit your social interaction or it will exhaust and irritate you, and you will give the impression of someone who has no social graces and who doesn't know how to behave.

# False advertising and window-dressing

There are good and bad motives for conscious impression management. Putting on a show doesn't have to mean getting involved in deceit, lies, exaggeration or conceal-ment. Window dressing: 'The use of physical changes in one's environment or appearance which makes a person appear more desirable' – may appear to be deceitful as the goal of this behaviour is to 'create the impression of greater prestige, wealth, competence or other socially desirable characteristics'. This strategy is commonly used when you've made the decision that you want your audience to see you at your best, when meeting decision makers, when making a sales pitch or socially, meeting your partner's parents for example.

It is possible to use deceitful manipulation to get what you want or to get out of trouble. Just because it's possible doesn't mean that everyone who consciously manages the impression they create is being deceitful. This is a facile interpretation of a complex and natural human activity.

## Three good reasons to make the effort

Research across a large number of organizations shows that three factors determine one's chances of promotion:

- Performance – 10 per cent
- Image and personal style – 30 per cent
- Exposure and visibility – 60 per cent.

If decisions about suitability for promotion or leadership are made partly on image and if everyone in the organization already works hard, then image and visibility become an issue and there are at least three reasons to make a good impression.

### 1. The power of personal impact

Many well-qualified and able people still go unrecognized because they put themselves and their ideas across badly and they underestimate the power of their personal style to influence judgements about their work. A typical career path today is not a series of logical upward steps rewarded by an annual increase in salary. Today, it is more likely to include working in teams or working on projects with different groups of people at different times, reinforcing the need for well-developed interpersonal skills and positive personal impact.

### 2. Visibility counts for more than ability

Being seen by the right people in the right places is more important than getting your head down and just accomplishing tasks. This means that in order to get on we need to develop our social skills. This includes interpersonal communication, networking and influencing skills – in order to be seen and remembered and to make a favourable impression on a daily basis.

### 3. Reflection of corporate image

People create the image of any organization. People are our first contact, whether it's a shop, a hospital or a restaurant . . . whether our first contact is over the phone, over the counter, or at the reception desk, this is our introduction to their corporate style. Wally Olins, creator of BT's logo, said that corporate image is 'the company's philosophy made visible through its people'. It's an internal as well as external activity. It shouldn't be about tarting the place up for the TV cameras when there's a crisis. We all know the kind of set-up where a fortune has been spent on everything from advertising to architecture, then they go and employ the receptionist from hell! You are always an ambassador for your firm.

## Dangerous advice

### 'Be yourself'

Yes, of course, you must be yourself but decide which role you will be playing and be your best professional self.

### 'Act natural'

Acting naturally is fine if your audience wants natural. If your natural style is the 'I'm too good for this place' kind of arrogance or its opposite in the form of a laid-back, don't-care attitude, the danger is that both of these styles could come across negatively; overconfidence can be seen as self-important and over-relaxed as spaced out.

## **Checkpoint**

| | |
|---|---|
| **Outcome** | What do I want to get out of the situation? |
| **Audience** | Who do I want to impress? Who is going to be there? What is the audience profile? |
| **Head** | What kind of planning, preparation or research will I have to do? |
| **Heart** | Will I have to do anything about my confidence level, my self-esteem or my nerves? |
| **Dress** | What image do I want to project? What shall I wear that does this? |
| **Voice** | Should I practise getting a particular tone to my voice? |
| **Body language** | What should I convey through my posture, gesture and mannerisms? |
| **Message** | What shall I say? Am I clear about the message I want to transmit? |

## 2

# HEAD AND HEART
## Using your brain and your emotions

Impression – *an effect produced (esp. on the mind or feelings)*
*a) impress – affect or influence deeply, evoke a favourable opinion or reaction from a person*
*b) a characteristic mark or quality*
The Concise Oxford Dictionary, 1990

They say you don't get a second chance to make a first impression. Even if this is not entirely true, it is true to say that it is very difficult to overcome a bad first impression. Making the right impression could be just luck but you increase your chances of success by taking control and managing the impression you want to create. Deciding to make the right impression in most everyday situations means that you are faced with social and intellectual decisions to make – what to wear, what to say, how to behave – as well as profound emotional states to deal with, controlling lack of self-esteem, attacks of nerves and over- or underconfidence. In a business situation we score each other consciously and unconsciously and rate the other person's professional impact.

## Inside

Once you have identified your target situation you start the process of making the right impression from the inside. Working with your head and your heart you use thought and emotion to identify what you want to get out of the situation, your personal goals or outcomes. You need to know who your target audience will be and who you want to impress. Once you know what you want and who you have to influence, you use your brain to think through a strategy and decide what research, information or pre-planning will be necessary. What is your emotional response to the situation coming up? What is your level of confidence and self-esteem like? Is what you're experiencing new for you or is it following a familiar pattern?

## Outside

This period of reflection and planning is followed by action. This means it's time to decide how you want to look, what kind of image you want to project and how you want to come across through the non-verbal channels of vocal tone and body language. The final external element is the verbal message you want to send and how you intend to say it. All the elements are important but as research shows that seven per cent of the impact is created by the words themselves then it doesn't pay to concentrate on that area and neglect the others.

These are the eight components which we'll look at in more detail in the following chapters:

- What you think
- The way you feel
- Your goal
- The audience
- How you look
- How you move
- How you sound
- What you say.

This chapter is about the head and heart – what you think and how you feel.

## What you think

This section is about the power that comes from planning, information and self-knowledge. Are you a planner and list-maker or do you prefer to take things as they come and let life happen? Do you prefer to take things step-by-step, being practical, deal with the facts – or do you like to look ahead at what might be, make connections, enjoy novelty? Do you make decisions with your head or your heart? It's not a question of a right or wrong attitude, it's more about being comfortable with your preference – your attitude to the world crossed with how you think about yourself.

> The extent to which you as an individual are prepared to monitor and adjust how you come across will influence the kind of impression you make.

## What you feel

Are you an outwardly confident person yet feel that one day the world will find you out as an imposter? Do you ever experience self-doubt or feel that your life is out of control? Even the most successful people will confess to being frightened that one day the bubble will burst and their unconfident and incompetent selves will be revealed. If we have self-esteem we have learnt not to have a constant fear of being found out but to be comfortable with our real selves. Self-esteem is built on:

- your right to be yourself
- honouring your skills and achievements
- channelling your energy in the best direction for you
- organizing your time fruitfully, doing what you want to do not what you ought to do.

If you don't appreciate yourself it will undoubtedly show on the outside through the way you look, the way you move and your tone of voice. If you respect yourself and are at ease with yourself you are a less demanding person, less needy of others and as result someone who projects a more positive impression of themselves. Do you know what you look like when your self-esteem is low? When you are under pressure? When things are not going your way? When you are angry or depressed? Maybe you frown, have agitated body movements, breathe too fast, stop listening, get sarcastic, focus on the problem not on the solution, switch off completely or withdraw. Any steps you take to increase your self-awareness in this area will pay off.

You can't hide neglect. If you haven't looked after your mind, your soul and spirit properly, it will show on the outside as it would if you had not looked after your body. Nurturing ourselves builds confidence but that confidence does sometimes seem to be built on shifting sands. A chance remark, a less than excellent presentation or a bad hair day can wipe out your confidence on the spot.

- Can you identify your personal 'boosters', the things that give you confidence?
- Can you identify your personal 'busters', the things that are likely to sap your confidence?
- Can you identify the currency you will need to buy in a confidence 'boost'?

> Whatever it costs in terms of time, personal relationships, money or effort to boost your confidence for a special occasion – if you need it, buy it, in whatever is the appropriate currency!

## Coping with nerves – recognition and rescue

When you get nervous the brain is sending signals to the body saying 'I can't do this . . .', 'I'll make a fool of myself . . .', 'I'm really frightened'. If an important occasion brings on an attack of nerves be grateful and next time it happens use the opportunity to recognize your symptoms. What did the brain do? What did the body do? How did you feel? Once you've recognized the symptoms you can learn to trigger a recovery mechanism. If you want to create the right impression the key lies in adequate and appropriate preparation for the situation.

> You know you've got it right when there is no discord between who you think you are and what you seem to be!

# Scenes

## Interviews

### Classic interview questions

One thing to get straight at this stage is that there are no 'right' answers out there in the same way that there are right answers to questions in a history exam. There are appropriate responses to be made that let the interviewer know what kind of person they are dealing with. It makes sense to rehearse responses to predictable questions which may be about your technical ability, your communication skills, recent achievements and past experience, or you might have to field questions designed to assess your level of self-awareness, solicit your views on current issues and test how you form opinions:

1. Why you? If we select you for the post what three things could you contribute?

2. Why us? What is it about this post that you find attractive?

3. Why now? How does this position fit into your long-term career plans? How do your plans fit with the strategic development of this organization?

4. Tell us about a significant challenge you have faced this year and what the results were?

5. What kind of management style gets the best out of you?

6. What frustrates you?

7. If we appoint you, how long would it take you to be effective?

8. How do you balance your work with other aspects of your life such as family?

9. Is there a saying that describes your philosophy?

10. If you had three wishes for the future of this industry/profession what would they be?

> **In order to make the right impression you must really want the job – not just the interview experience!**

## Meetings

Meetings can act as a showcase for your professional style. They are also an opportunity to practise your communication skills and are a way of both being visible and having your style judged. If you learn to think strategically about meetings you can use them as a vehicle to develop your communication style, present your ideas and influence and manage people. Control your contribution. Control your feelings. Plan what you want to say and don't let yourself be intimidated by loud, offensive or well-polished contributors.

### The first-time Chair

Poor Chairing skills can allow the meeting to run out of time, to let issues go unresolved, to neglect to make key decisions, to make people feel their contribution has gone unrewarded and to allow participants to insult each other.

1. Have a clear purpose for the meeting.

2. Be the best-prepared and best-informed person in the group. You can't Chair a meeting effectively and take notes at the same time. Delegate note-taking to a volunteer.

3. Don't meet unless you have to. Regular meetings are pointless unless there is regular news and regular decisions to be taken that can't happen any other way.

4. Limit the numbers.

5. Communicate the objectives, framework and timing.

6. Encourage participation.

7. Stay on the strategic path if possible and save the detail for working parties.

8. Give the background to items or speakers that might be unfamiliar to the group.

9. Summarize at the end of each item. Clarify action to be taken and by whom.

10. Don't allow 'action replay'. If someone missed the previous meeting or meetings and wants to go over an issue again, be firm, don't allow it.

11. Talk to people between meetings. Build bridges.

## Presentations

### Prepare your material

Whether you have 30 seconds or 30 minutes you won't make a good impression with your presentation unless you have done some preparation. Even very experienced speakers will tell you they had a plan even if it was on the back of their hand minutes before they spoke. If you haven't written it down, then the thoughts and ideas which have been going round in your mind for days before the event will be lost. Successful speakers make it look easy, that's their charm.

### Get in the mood

Put yourself in presentation mood while you are still on the way to the event. Don't leave getting properly dressed to when you are in the car or in the cloakroom. Use everyone you meet on the way to rehearse the picture you want to

21

present of your best professional self – on the tube, in the car, in the car park, at reception, in the lift – your body language will be exhibiting confident signals all the way there.

## Plan for making a 10-minute presentation

Answer these key questions before you even begin to consider the content:

- Am I clear about what I want to get out of the situation?

- Have I identified my audience – who will be there, what are their expectations?

- How much time have I got?

- Where will it be?

- What exactly is the subject matter?

Concentrate on the 93 per cent we know forms the initial impact; look the part, rehearse the appropriate body language and cope with any nerves. Then put your mental energy into the content. This is not an argument for style over content, just a practical plan for getting important information across to the maximum number of people while maintaining their interest and respect. This plan is based on the time factor of 10 minutes. In a short presentation, ie up to about 20 minutes, every second counts. Saying good morning, and telling the audience what you're going to be talking about could use up your 10 minutes if you aren't disciplined and haven't got a plan.

To make it interesting for everyone in the audience try to provide a range of ways of illustrating your material. Each topic and sub-topic should be illustrated differently for maximum effect. Use a mixture of stories, anecdotes, data, charts, photos, cartoons, newspaper quotes, scientific research and so on. Draw from a wide range of subjects; history, geography, literature, politics, sport and entertainment.

# 3

# AUDIENCE AND OUTCOMES
## Who will be there and what you want to get out of the situation

You are more likely to make the right impression when you are very clear what you want to get out of the situation. This chapter will help you to identify your goals and the nature of your audience. Time spent clarifying your outcomes and expectations is never wasted. Mixing fantasy and reality, having a good imagination, keeping the mind open to accept the unexpected and being something of an opportunist will make the process more dynamic and interesting.

## Your goal

Goal-setting is effective if it meets six criteria:

1. Specific rather than general – several small goals are easier to reach than one big broad aim: 'I'd like to be better known by the Chairman and Membership Secretary then get on the committee at the Squash Club, then be the Press Officer' works better than 'I want to be famous!'

2. Realistic

3. Relevant – life moves on, fashion changes as do our personal and professional circumstances

4. Action-orientated

5. Targeted to a date

6. Control is more with you than with outside forces.

Being clear about your goals is not always easy. It helps to break down the situation into small pieces and ask some key questions. All the questions won't be relevant to all situations and it may take several attempts to get to the right answers.

- Why am I doing this?
- What do I want to get out of it?
- What could stop me?
- What will I have to *do* to achieve it?
- Who might I need to get on board?
- What resources might I need?
- Who might hinder the outcome?
- What are the likely hurdles or obstacles?
- Have I chosen the right vehicle to achieve my goal?
- Have I got the right audience to achieve my goal?

25

All the questions are important but we will concentrate on the first three questions:

# Why am I doing this?

There is usually a simple reason why you present yourself to an audience. Tick one or more reasons:

☐ Because I have to
  'Part of my job is to make presentations about new financial products to the customer care team.'

☐ To increase my credibility
  'Now I've got an MBA, I'd like to demonstrate my new insights to my colleagues and my boss.'

☐ To be more popular
  'People who try to get out of the team presentations are really disliked. I'm going to make more of an effort to contribute'

☐ To influence the right people
  'I'd like to show the people who are picking the new project team that I'm right for the job.'

☐ To prove a point
  'I've always said you can make finance attractive to non-financial managers. This presentation will prove it to them and the rest of the finance team.'

☐ I want to do the right thing
  'I'd like to hit the right note with my speech as best man, not too boring for my friends, not too racy for the old folks.'

☐ It will be professionally advantageous.
  'I would like to have my research paper accepted at the next academic conference so that I'm seen as a serious contributor to my specialism.'

# What do I want to get out of it?

- ☐ To keep my self-esteem intact
- ☐ To get a promotion
- ☐ To get a job
- ☐ To be seen to do the right thing
- ☐ To build my confidence
- ☐ To test my abilities
- ☐ To get some practice
- ☐ To be more assertive
- ☐ To be better known within the profession

# What could stop me?

It's natural to feel fear or anxiety when on unfamiliar territory, we all do. There are sound self-preservation instincts at work but if you don't take a bit of a risk, make mistakes and learn from them you'll have nothing on which to build a future.

## Fear

- Fear of failure – fear of success
- Fear of beginnings – fear of endings

## Procrastination

- 'I'll do it when . . .
- . . . I am slimmer
- . . . I've got more information
- . . . I feel stronger
- . . . we've redecorated the kitchen.'

Go back and answer the other questions when you have time.

> The clearer the objectives, the more easily you will be able to seize an opening or recognize opportunities when they present themselves.

## The audience

When I talk about an 'audience' I mean anyone that you want to impress, anyone who is going to be on the receiving end of your thoughts, feelings, image, behaviour and communication style. You can't make the right impression on anyone if you're too frightened to face your audience. Audiences become less scary when you know a bit about them. Whether it's one person or a dozen or thousands of people you need to draw up a profile of them so that you can match your efforts to their expectations.

### Audience profile

Build an audience profile by collecting information about its size, composition, prior knowledge and propensity. You can use this information to assess the situation. One way is to work through a list of opposite characteristics:

| | |
|---|---|
| Hostile | Friendly |
| Decision makers | Information seekers |
| Entertainment | Sales pitch |
| Purely social | Definitely business only |
| All specialists | General knowledge |
| They all know each other | All strangers |
| High profile | Low profile |
| Small and friendly | Large and impersonal |

Or you can start to build a profile by asking these kinds of questions:

- Who is going to be there, their names and job descriptions?
- How many of them will there be?
- What is their age range?
- Will there be men and women?
- A heterogeneous or varied mix?
- What is their level of seniority?
- What are their expectations?
- What specialist knowledge do they have?
- Do they want to be there?
- Do they have any prejudices?
- Do they have any strong religious or political beliefs?
- Why should they want to listen to me?
- Are they like me or not like me?

When time is short, go over the audience profile and check three areas that will be the most significant, then build your presentation round one or all those. For example:

- If they are specialists in the same subject as you – concentrate on getting your facts straight and have something special up your sleeve, new information, surprising facts, be ready to flatter them and ask them for their views

- If it is a large and impersonal group who may not know each other, share a personal anecdote, be a bit larger than life, include the audience by asking rhetorical questions or posing imaginary problems for them to solve.

- Learn to flex your style and to be aware of the need to adapt it to different audiences.
- Learn not to be disappointed when the audience doesn't love your style even when the content and technical delivery are sound.
- Whatever your subject do your best to make it interesting – people love anecdotes and pictures as well as receiving the hard data.

Consider the relationship between image and audience. Your image takes on reality only when it has an audience to respond to it, even if it's only an audience of one. In self-marketing terms your potential audience is vast – the whole of the world of work. If you want to create the right impression you should monitor your image constantly.

## Internal and external audience

There is usually an internal as well as an external audience to be considered. The internal audience is your inner voice. It could be your best professional self that you want to live up to or it could be your former headteacher who had low expectations of you at school. Your external audience might be just one person, your boss, for example, at your appraisal meeting, or several hundred people at your first conference presentation.

## Difficult customers

Why do some people have to make your life uncomfortable when they act as your audience? It's as though they were genetically programmed to ask the most awkward question, to sit with a disapproving look glued to their faces, to interrupt, to be sarcastic or undermine your efforts.

Maybe they're bored, they're attention-seeking, showing off their own knowledge or skills, want to put you right on a matter of fact, set off on rambling questions or want to put their own concerns on your agenda. It might help you to make the right impression to consider tactics for dealing with them:

- Don't retaliate
- Don't argue
- Stay polite
- Don't panic
- Ask them to repeat the question/criticism/objection
- Don't make a promise you can't keep just to get out of the situation.

> If things are not going well, consider whether or not it's you who is being difficult.

## Scenes

### New job

### Twenty-two negative impressions

If you fail to take audience response into account and are disinclined to modify your behaviour, you may like to consider this list of common 'turn-offs' in communal business life.

1. Smoking in no-smoking areas
2. Chewing gum (at any time except when you haven't got an audience) makes you look vacant and stupid

3. Grazing at your desk – continually snacking on fizzy drinks, crisps, biscuits and sweets

4. Pinning up 'amusing' slogans of the – 'You don't have to be mad to work here – but it helps!' variety

5. Eating breakfast at your desk or at a meeting

6. Old coffee cups, plastic beakers or cans left lying about

7. Turning up late

8. Reading non-work material, eg a novel, magazine or newspaper at your desk

9. Sportsbags

10. Plastic carrier bags

11. Cuddly toys

12. Yawning

13. Moaning all the time

14. Shouting or laughing very loudly

15. Complaining about a hangover

16. A very tidy desk

17. A very untidy desk

18. Too many family photos, pictures or postcards surrounding your desk or work area

19. Girlie magazines or nude photos pinned up

20. Hogging the phone/fax for private calls

21. Not saying 'hello' when you arrive in the morning

22. Refusing to take messages for people when they aren't at their desk

## Presentations

In 30 minutes you can do two things that will make a huge difference to any presentation and help you to create a favourable impression:

## 1. Be clear what you expect to get out of the situation and be just as clear about what your audience can expect

Define your audience and who will need to be impressed early on. What effect do you want to have on them? What effect do you want to achieve?

- To educate them
- To inform them
- To entertain them
- To persuade them
- To shock them
- To frighten them
- To sell to them

Getting this straight means that you can quickly move on to other decisions about style and content. I once asked a client what her definition of a professional presentation was. She replied: 'One where the presenter is well-dressed and well-prepared; knows their material and is an enthusiast; has a clear brief which is communicated to the audience and starts and finishes on time!'

## 2. Personalize your presentations to appeal to the audience of the moment

- Even if it's the same material for a different audience in a different venue, resist the temptation to roll out the same old stuff which may come across as cold and insincere. Obviously you don't say it if you don't mean it: 'I have happy memories of the last time I was in Oxford . . .'; It's a pleasure to be back in Manchester, I can always be sure of a warm welcome . . .'

- Remember the WIIFM factor (What's In It For Me). The earlier in your presentation you can explain exactly why the audience should listen to you and why it is important to them, the more likely they are to listen attentively.

- Whatever your topic give your audience what they want. Include one or two of the major motivators such as: peer group approval, financial security, the opportunity to be the best, to be the first, to be creative, to have their efforts recognized, to accomplish something worth while, to have more control over their destiny. It takes a little skill and a little more imagination to weave in a life motivator into a presentation called 'Business Process Re-engineering – the way forward' but it will definitely be worth the sweat.

# 4

# HOW YOU LOOK
# Body talk and the
# language of clothes

*Clothing is the furniture of the mind made visible.*

James Laver

Non-verbal communication is a powerful form of behaviour and acts a gatekeeper to the emotions and perceptions of other people. Body talk and the language of clothes reach us on an instinctive level that does not require effort of speech or intellect.

## Body talk

You can talk with your body through the way you move, sit, stand and walk before you speak a word. There is a range of informal to formal body language. The most effective way of communicating is by appearing relaxed but alert

– you will exude confidence and control. Too relaxed and people will feel you do not care about them, only yourself. If your body is stiff and static you are communicating hostility and insecurity. Making the right impression includes the following aspects of non-verbal behaviour.

- **Eye contact**: The ability to make and maintain eye contact looks confident; lowering the eyes appears submissive or flirtatious depending on the context.

- **Smile**: Eye contact and a smile are appropriate in all but the gravest of situations. A smile can convey warmth, show confidence and establish rapport. An inappropriate smile can also give out a mixed message if it is combined with an angry tone of voice or when you are hoping to be taken seriously. Smiling at the wrong moment can project weakness, a lack of assertiveness or can be interpreted as flirting.

- **Looking down your nose**: If you habitually hold your head up and tipped slightly back when you look at someone, you appear to be looking down your nose at them and so come across as aloof or superior. Some people who wear glasses do this. If you can see without them, it gives a better impression to take your glasses off when you talk to people.

- **Posture**: The way you sit, stand and walk can make you appear confident, brash, timid, healthy or under the weather. A confident demeanour is recognizable in someone who 'walks tall'.

- **Gesture**: Gestures can add warmth to a cold style of communication. Some cultures use more gestures and hand movements than others. Suppose everyone in your family talks with their hands then someone who limits their hand gestures could seem cold or uncommunicative to you. Gestures can be used in two ways:

**To emphasize** – hand gestures can add emphasis in the same way that print can – <u>underline</u>, **bold**, *italic*

**To describe** – to show the length, width, height or scale of an object or person.

**Unconscious and conscious gestures**
Gestures such as waving, blowing a kiss or making a rude sign are conscious actions. Ear-tugging, neck-scratching or hair-twiddling are done unconsciously and we have little control over them. It is these gestures that are sometimes referred to as 'negative leakage' and are said to speak the truth when the words we speak are lies.

■ **Facial expression**: Your face has the ability to show all the basic human emotions – fear, anger, happiness surprise and so on. Some people have marvellously expressive faces while other faces remain a mask. Do you know how your own face expresses emotion?

■ **Eyebrow flash**: Flashing your eyebrows up for a second when you meet someone is a sign of friendship.

■ **Nodding**: If you nod your head while someone is talking to you they might think you are agreeing with them but really you are just saying 'go on, I'm still listening'.

■ **Territory and positioning**: Our sense of personal space is very important to us. We are aware of an invisible defensive zone or personal space that surrounds us and feel uncomfortable if another person invades our space. There are cultural and temperamental differences in the amount of space we prefer to put between ourselves and others. In some cultures standing close up, hugging and touching are normal. The tendency in British business culture is to keep further apart.

- **Touch**: People who have a 'warm' social style and constantly lean in towards you and touch your arm or thigh can be seen as flirtatious, condescending or over-friendly in a business context. In business circles touching is therefore limited to a handshake.

> Body language is a two-way street. It tells us how you feel and think about yourself and how you feel and think about others.

## The language of clothes

The way you look does matter. People I talk to about image and dress often confess to insecurities about how they should 'design' themselves for a prospective audience. Whether they are thinking of the audience that they face every day made up of colleagues at work or the occasional high profile public presentation, they are confused and insecure about what choices to make from an ever-increasing range of possibilities. This is a particularly spiky problem for women who already face prejudice and don't want to appear unsophisticated or ignorant by making the wrong choice. Research conducted for *The Independent* showed that 80 per cent of people surveyed thought that women who were not wearing jackets were receptionists or secretaries.

### Interference

Clothing is a form of communication which sends and receives information and as such sometimes suffers from a 'bad line'. Classic examples of interference are:

- **Past experience**: Your mother always wore a silk scarf inside her coat at the neckline therefore anyone who wears a scarf in the same way must be over 60 like she is

- **Social factors**: Wearing head-to-toe black to a traditional church wedding in the UK wouldn't be admired however gorgeous you looked

- **Cultural differences**: Confirmation dresses of the type worn by little Catholic girls on the Continent seem overdressed to low church

- **Infatuation**: If you are in love then the beloved will seem beautiful a chip wrapper

- **Indifference**: If you have fallen out of love with someone they become invisible, so the way they look is irrelevant.

## Like attracts like

The picture that is formed by the outfit someone puts together communicates to us before a word is spoken. When we meet someone who is dressed in a style similar to our own we infer that they will have similar attitudes, beliefs and values to our own. Try this experiment. Next time you are with a group of strangers, for example at an external training course, if you find that there is one person you get on with better than the others, take a critical look at what they are wearing. How closely does it mirror your choice? Not necessarily the same garments but a similar 'look'. People who get on well often share the same way of putting a look together. If, indeed, like attracts like then you will be more inclined to want to do business together.

Today, men's clothes are becoming more colourful and womenswear for business is less formal and tailored. Even so, people in business, particularly in traditional areas of retail, finance or manufacturing, can be suspicious of an unusual form of dress. It creates an immediate barrier which might make the other person less receptive of what you have to say. For example, if you arrive at a team Awayday wearing a Hawaiian shirt and shorts and everyone else is in usual business dress you could be creating the impression that:

■ you have just returned from holiday and your luggage is still in Hawaii

■ as usual, you are expressing your flamboyant personality through bright colours and casual styles

■ the programme did stress that the Awayday would be informal.

## 'You are what you wear'

It may be illogical to connect the way we look with who we are but we all do it all the same. What impression do you want to create? Is there a gap between your vision and the reality? Start on the inside again and consider your attitude to clothes and image. Where would you position yourself on the clothes line:

---

Expressive ←  → Neutral ←  → Functional

---

■ **Expressive**: Enjoys clothes and uses clothes to express mood and feelings; considers dress to be an art form.

■ **Neutral**: Simply obeys social rules, dresses to a budget, not stylish or smart.

■ **Functional**: Chooses outfits to match what they have to do. May or may not get pleasure from the activity.

## What kind of image do you want to project?

It's asking too much of the same outfit, hairstyle and accessories to project different images according to the situation, so it is necessary to fine-tune the business wardrobe to be more adaptable. For example a tailored pink jacket worn with a short navy skirt and row of pearls might look conservative but businesslike for an interview. Team the same jacket with cream trousers, strappy shoes and contemporary jewellery and you have a more modern upbeat look for a sales conference.

## The ideal outfit

The most successful outfit for any occasion, business or social, formal or casual, will project the image that you want and:

- Be flattering
- Be comfortable
- Give you confidence
- Reflect your personality
- Reflect the social dress code
- Support your message.

> To make the right impression you have to find the balance between what you prefer and what is necessary. It's a wonderful day when preference and necessity are a perfect match.

## Scenes

### Meetings

### What makes you look nervous

- Taking earrings on and off
- Running chain round neck or finger round chain
- Twirling wedding or engagement ring
- Twiddling hair round your finger
- Clicking your pen
- Jangling loose change in your pocket
- Examining long hair for split ends
- Straightening paper clips
- Pushing glasses up the nose
- Rubbing your tummy
- Frequently licking your lips

### Powerful mannerisms

- Don't fumble through your paperwork while you speak. You'll look disorganized and give out signals that it's OK to interrupt you.
- To interrupt someone else or make a point, make direct eye contact with speaker or Chair, take off glasses or earrings, raise hand, pen or finger, palm up.
- Lean forward, hands on table, own the space.

### Interviews

### Guidelines for a 'safe' interview outfit

- ✓ Find out what the expectations are and meet them. Play a part and get the costume
- ✓ Clean lines – avoid droopy or frilly lines

✓ Uncluttered neck and shoulder line

✓ Neutral or subdued colours for main garments: for example, navy, grey, black, or pine green, aubergine, rust, taupe, a brighter coloured or pastel jacket is OK for women but not coloured skirt or shoes

✓ No pattern in main garments

✓ Nothing sleeveless

✓ Classic styling – nothing exaggerated

✓ No boots or sandals

✓ Good grooming

✓ No perfume or aftershave

✓ Women – wear tights, a little make-up, avoid trousers, avoid long bright-red nails

✓ Men – close shave, socks long enough to avoid expanse of leg when you sit down, tie should be interesting not 'funny', don't wear a short-sleeved shirt with a tie or a business suit, don't wear a jumper under your jacket

✓ Play one wild card, eg very long or very short hair, stylish glasses, designer shoes

✓ Present yourself at your professional best so that, even if you are not appointed, you leave the interviewers with a favourable impression

## Presentations

Match your non-verbals to the verbals. Consider what type of presentation it is going to be and what the atmosphere and audience will be like. If you are good at reading the situation, you can move through both styles (set out below) if necessary, according to the response from the audience and the content of the message.

| Informal | Formal |
|---|---|
| **Achieved by** | **Achieved by** |
| Sitting on edge of table | Standing upright |
| Moving away from lectern or table | Remaining at lectern |
| Walking about | Standing still |
| Leaning against lectern | Body away from lectern |
| Hands in pockets | Hands resting on sides of lectern |
| Plenty of hand gestures | Few gestures |
| Taking off jacket, loosening tie | Jacket buttoned up |
| **Effective for** | **Effective for** |
| Workshops | Junior to senior |
| Facilitating, not lecturing | Conveying authority |
| Senior to junior | Conveying strength |
| Establishing a friendly atmosphere | Serious situation |
| Appearing relaxed | Hostile audience |

## New job

1. Check guidelines for employee dress in the employee handbook.

2. Find out for yourself by asking the person who will be your boss.

3. Before the first day, visit the site and observe other employees, particularly those of your age and status.

4. If in doubt play it safe and stick to a conservative look – you can show your personal style later on.

5. Don't take sandwiches in a box on the first day – you'll look like a nerd.

6. If you intend to wear your interview/graduation suit, check that it still fits you.

# 5

# HOW YOU SOUND AND WHAT YOU SAY
## Voice and message

### How you sound

It's not what you say, it's the way that you say it. The vocal tone or 'shape' of your voice conveys 38 per cent of your message. We convey active emotions such as happiness or anger by speaking louder, faster and with a higher pitch. In contrast, passive emotion such as boredom, sadness, or depression is conveyed by speaking more softly and slowly with a lower pitch and less intonation. We have all the richness of the voice available to help make the right impression. There are many elements that contribute to our unique vocal style including:

- Style of delivery
- Pitch
- Pace

- Pause
- Clarity
- Accent
- Volume
- Fluency
- Breathing.

Prepare to make a good impression by checking out the 'shape' of your voice and considering each of its component parts.

- **Delivery**: An aspect of self-awareness that is useful to notch up is to recognize your style of verbal and vocal delivery. The effect of your style will influence the outcome of all sorts of situations, not just in big set-piece presentations or when delivering a training programme but also when contributing to a meeting or creative ideas session. Do you only have one style of delivery or can you adapt your style to the circumstances? Where would you place yourself on the delivery line?

> Quiet reasonableness → → → → Erupting volcano

- **Pitch**: Determine where your natural vocal range is pitched. You'll have to listen to yourself on a tape recorder. Of course it won't sound like the voice you hear in your head but there will be enough information to tell you where your voice is pitched compared to the next person who speaks to you or you hear on the television.

> Low pitch → → → → High pitch

| Assertive | Nervous |
|-----------|---------|
| In control | Afraid |
| Credibility | Lost control |
| Authority | Over-excited |

We are inclined to associate the higher notes with tension: too high and we risk loss of credibility; too shrill and we think we hear loss of control. I've never come across a public figure criticized because their voice is pitched too low.

■ **Pace**: The average rate of speech is about 100–120 words per minute. A rapid pace is sometimes seen as an indication of a quick mind and a slow pace with no pauses can seem dull and boring even if the content is good. Some people speak quickly if they're nervous, to get it over with. The perception is that they have nothing to contribute.

Try this exercise. Write out 300–400 words and time how long it takes to read them or speak them naturally. If you can count more than 120 words per minute check whether you are gabbling, not pausing for breath, not enunciating clearly. If so, you might come across as bright but what's the point if no one can follow your flow of ideas.

■ **Pause**: Pauses in the right places add a dynamic to the spoken word. They can add drama, poignancy or be used for emphasis. Some people are frightened of pausing in case they get interrupted or lose the flow, so they fill the gap with 'ums' or 'ers' or 'if you see what I mean . . .' The long drawn out 'er' is an arrogant way of keeping the audience waiting while you collect your thoughts. Frequent 'ums' or 'ers' are irritating and suggest you may not know what you are talking about or that you have not prepared what you want to say. Pausing and living with the ensuing silence is a powerful indicator of confidence.

- **Clarity**: Someone once said: 'If you look after the consonants, the vowels will take care of themselves'. It doesn't matter how brilliant your thoughts are if you can't articulate them clearly without mumbling. If you mumble you create a distance between you and the other person; you don't allow them into your vocal space. If your speech is lazy and indistinct it conveys arrogance or lack of commitment and energy.

- **Accent**: Your accent is by no means a barrier to making the right impression. What counts is clarity – clarity of diction, pronunciation and meaning. In the UK the most socially acceptable accent and the least regionally limiting if you have a national audience is still BBC English or Received Standard Pronunciation. Surveys show that strong regional accents, particularly those from Birmingham, Belfast, Glasgow, Liverpool and London Cockney are not popular out of their own area. Should you move away from the accent you were brought up with? There is no reason, other than you are more likely to increase your impact if your message is clearly understood by as wide an audience as possible.

- **Volume**: Remember the volume control. Turn it up or down as necessary. If your voice is too loud you may seem aggressive, overconfident or nervous and inexperienced, unable to monitor your projection. Too soft a voice also sounds nervous but can seem weak, suggest that you are not very well or that you are inexperienced and lack self-awareness of how your voice comes across. A more positive perception of a soft voice is that the speaker is gentle and not aggressive.

- **Fluency**: Hesitancy in speech could indicate lack of knowledge of the subject, or an unwillingness to speak. Compete sentences rather than unfinished, half-formed sentences give an impression of elegant thoughts.

- **Look after your voice**: Breathe through your nose and take in warmed air. Take in liquids but not milk, or milk in coffee or tea, which has the effect of thickening your saliva and may make your voice 'crack'. Other dairy products such as cheese, cream, or ice-cream can also have this effect.

## What you say

Being able to speak well in public is a social and business asset. Try to build a reputation as someone who talks well across a desk or at meetings. Powerful and memorable entrance and exit lines are what you concentrate on if you don't have much time.

## Entrances

1. **Tell a funny story or tell a joke**
   Tell a joke only if you do it elegantly and we didn't all hear it on TV last night.

2. **Tell a powerful story**
   I was doing a presentation called 'The Image Factor' on the day the media ran a story about an American tourist who had been refused admission to Harrods because her clothing was not appropriate – a gift of an opening.

3. **Relevant quotation**
   Shakespeare and the Bible are a never-ending source of good openers.

### 4. Compliment the audience
Paying the audience a genuine compliment about their success, their creativity, their hospitality.

### 5. Ask a challenging question
At an internal corporate communication conference I heard the Chief Executive get instant attention by asking: 'How many of you think that allocating a new budget to internal communication is a waste of time?'.

### 6. Surprising statistics
'One in five university undergraduates do not have the basic communication skills employers need.' An attention-grabbing way to start a talk to students about job opportunities.

### 7. Surprise opening
Play a tape of Gloria Gaynor singing 'I will survive' to a group of people thinking about giving up their profession to become entrepreneurs.

## Exits

### 1. Surprise ending
Sometimes memorability is a more important outcome than the message. I have closed with a tap-dance, a strip-tease and a song (not all in the same presentation) in order that the audience would remember me not just the message.

### 2. Safe ending
Clearly summarize your key points.

### 3. Quotation
A neat technique is to dovetail your close with your opening quotation.

### 4. Joke or funny story
This is a good close if you can carry it off and the occasion is not over-formal.

### 5. End in an upbeat way
An inspiring or uplifting message is needed on some occasions.

### 6. Ask for positive action
'When you leave the lecture theatre today I'd like to ask those of you who don't already have their own copy to buy my latest book.'

### 7. Ask a direct question
'If we don't intervene now, what hope is there for our future relationship with the Council?'

### 8. Pay a compliment
'It's been a marvellous occasion and I can't wait for the next time!'

### 9. Give two options for action in the form of a question
'Shall we give up now or let the competition know we intend to fight? The choice is yours.'

## What to avoid

- **Giving offence**: Maintain gender neutrality and avoid racist remarks

- **Off colour jokes**: If you tell a good story you can still do so but leave the dirty jokes for single sex gatherings

- **Referring to ladies, girls or chicks**: 'Women' is a better bet

- **Jargon:** Unless you are 100 per cent sure your audience shares the vocabulary

- **Euphemisms**: Say what you mean
- **Swearing**: Never at a public presentation
- **Fillers**: One way to spoil an effective message is to package it between disclaimers or softeners:

  '. . . as far as I know'

  '. . . it's only my opinion but . . .'

  'Time may prove me wrong but . . .'

  '. . . so to speak'

  '. . . as it were'

  'I could be mistaken but . . .'

Try adding a softener to 'Football is not about life or death – it's more important than that'. It might turn out this way: 'It's only my opinion, but football is not about life or death – it's so to speak more important than that!' Add a disclaimer to any of the memorable statements of this century: Martin Luther King's 'I have a dream . . .' or 'The lady's not for turning!' from Margaret Thatcher . . .

> . . . and listen to them fade.

## Make a good impression on the phone

When we use the phone we have to do without the visual clues that give the advantage of face-to-face communication. Making the right impression over the phone includes listening as well as talking. If you smile when you speak it makes the tone more pleasant. If you want to sell an idea or when you want to sound enthusiastic or want to be more assertive and give yourself a bolt of courage – stand up!

## Remember your telephone manners

- Make it a rule to return all incoming calls within 24 hours at the outside.
- Try to answer on the second or third ring – after the first ring is too sudden and doesn't give callers enough time to compose themselves.
- Avoid taking calls when you have someone with you.
- Always call for a reason not just a chat.
- Make a list of the points you want to cover before you call. Have the relevant file open on the computer or have the paperwork to hand.

## Scenes

### Interviews

- Use the vocabulary from any psychometric tests you may have done, eg describe your leadership style or your team member profile.
- Be able to use anecdotes and be willing to prove through illustration, argument and example what you can do and how you can achieve results.
- Have evidence ready of how you would go about tackling what is unfamiliar.
- Demonstrate how you could hit the deck running.
- Show a real interest in the organization and its business future.
- Rehearse your 'credo'. What do you believe in. What are your values?
- Rehearse an elegant and believable 30-second self-marketing statement. (Say what makes you a good choice for the job and why you'd like the opportunity to get it.)

## Meetings

### Powerful talk

- Don't whinge.
- Don't waffle.
- Don't start with an apology.
- Introduce yourself properly.

If you've been invited to attend a meeting for the first time don't blow an opportunity to make a good impression. Be prepared to introduce yourself in a proper professional way so that your body language and speech give the same message of control. Don't give your audience the chance to infer that you are not important, too junior for the role or otherwise incompetent by fluffing or fidgeting and throwing the introduction away: 'Oh, er . . . I'm Tim, I wasn't expecting to have to do this. Still here goes. I'm Tim, as I said and I'm in admin and I sort of do a bit everything really'. A crisper, more professional approach could be: 'My name is Tim, Tim Andrews. My background is in organizing exhibitions and I handle all the administrative support for the company's off-site training. I'm pleased to be here today.' Trying to gain the sympathy vote will not usually work. You say 'I hope this isn't going to be too boring', they hear 'This is going to be boring, very boring.'

## Presentations

Making a short presentation

| | | | |
|---|---|---|---|
| **Total time available:** | | | |
| **Audience:** | | | |
| **The subject:** | | | |
| **Desired outcome:** | | | |
| | **Time** | **Script** | **Examples** |
| **Entrance and opening remarks** | ½ min | | |
| **Introduction** | 1½ min | | |
| **Topic A:** **point 1** | 1 min | | |
| **point 2** | 1 min | | |
| **Topic B:** **point 1** | 1 min | | |
| **point 2** | 1 min | | |
| **Topic C:** **point 1** | 1 min | | |
| **point 2** | 1 min | | |
| **Summary** | 1 min | | |
| **Conclusion** | ½ min | | |
| **Exit line** | ½ min | | |
| **Total:** | **10 min** | | |

# 6

# THE SOCIAL SCENE

There's no doubt that your social and interpersonal skills will count for just as much as your technical and business skills if you want to make a good impression. A promising career can be wrecked if you don't know how to behave in social situations. You weren't recruited for your social skills were you? Maybe not but you can't escape the fact that if you want to get on, you'll need ready access to a range of social graces.

Have you noticed that some people wherever they go, manage to leave behind a positive impression of themselves as a guest. Not everyone is a natural extrovert, loves meeting people and because of their personality, education or background, always seems to know the right thing to say and do. If you're not sure how you measure up socially, try these questions:

1. Your boss pops into your office where you are having a meeting with a client and several colleagues from other departments. How should the introductions be handled?

2. If you have invited someone to join you for a business lunch in a restaurant, when should you arrive?

   (a) half an hour before the agreed time

   (b) ten minutes before the agreed time

   (c) on time

   (d) a little late, a few minutes after your guest

3. What do you do if you've made a fool of yourself the previous evening and have been sick over or insulted your hostess?

4. The company you have just joined has a reputation for out-of-hours socializing. As a shy person you don't know whether to:

   (a) pretend to be more sociable than you really are

   (b) avoid going

   (c) do the minimum for appearance's sake

   (d) look for another job

(Answers at the end of this chapter on p. 63).

## Self-awareness

How many of the following situations have you experienced? Which ones did you find difficult? Which do you avoid?

- Christmas party
- Conference
- Drinks after work
- Drinks parties
- Making a speech
- Formal dinner
- Dinner in a restaurant

- Hot date with someone new
- Visiting boring relations
- Visiting your partner's family
- Entertaining foreign visitors to your firm

Why was the situation uncomfortable for you? Is it because you are the sort of person who is comfortable meeting people on a one-to-one basis but dislike being with a crowd or in the spotlight? Maybe you have some sympathy with Victor Kiam (the man who liked Remington shavers so much he bought the company) who said 'I don't party much. I don't enjoy talking to people that you're never going to see again about things you don't care about'. Some frequently occurring reasons why people don't enjoy these situations are listed here. Tick any that apply to you.

☐ I won't know anyone
☐ I won't know what to say
☐ I don't know what to wear
☐ I will have to play a part
☐ The other people are stupid, aggressive, better off, boring, only have one topic of conversation
☐ I might have to be nice to people I don't like
☐ I'll have to behave myself
☐ I don't like having to introduce people to each other
☐ I don't like pushing myself forward

Once you have identified the kind of occasions that you don't enjoy, and tried to work out why you don't enjoy them, this information positions you to design your own Social Situations Strategy – or SSS.

## Being self-centred

There is one common explanation why people don't create a good impression in social situations – SELF. The same underlying factor can result in opposing behaviour.

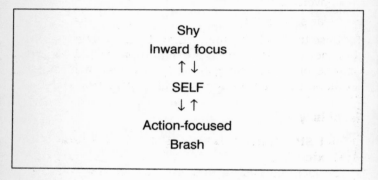

Shy
Inward focus
↑ ↓
SELF
↓ ↑
Action-focused
Brash

The common thread for shyness or brashness is that people obey their own instincts and preferences and do not take account of other people's needs or the demands of the occasion. If you earnestly want to make a good impression both kinds of behaviour can cause problems.

## Do you know anyone like this?

### The social dyslexic

Often brilliant at technical analysis, hopeless with people. They can be socially awkward and don't know the right things to do or say; also, more importantly, they have never grasped the need to. People like this are likely to:

- Do the wrong thing
- Laugh at the wrong moment
- Find small talk an agony

- Make inappropriate remarks, which drop like bricks but they don't notice
- Interrupt a conversation inappropriately
- Tell a story that has no relevance to the rest of the conversation
- Wear silly clothes.

Because they lack the ability to read others people's behaviour they can't interpret facial expression or body language or tone of voice. They can't tune in to the main message let alone the nuances of non-verbal expression.

## Is this you?

### Social Situations Strategy (SSS) for a social dyslexic

If you lack the kind of intuition that enables you to read non-verbal messages, learn to watch and listen very carefully for common social cues that will trigger the correct response. For example: 'How are you? I understand you've not been well recently'. Unless the question comes from your mother the answer is: 'Yes, but I'm fine now thanks. How are you?' It is not considered acceptable to talk about the details of constipation or your productive chesty cough.

The bonus of being with this kind of person is that once they trust you and like you they are a loyal friend and at work they do work hard and are not easily distracted.

## The kid in a sweetshop

Typically a cheerful, optimistic kind of person with a high energy quotient. They love challenge and change and newness. They can be perceived as dizzy, a show-off, with no depth to their character and insensitive to the needs of others. People like this are likely to:

- Be easily distracted
- Have trouble focusing their attention
- Live for the moment
- Crave excitement
- Leave a trail of unfinished projects
- Be hyperactive

## Is this you?

## Social Situations Strategy (SSS) for a kid in a sweetshop

Recognize your aptitude for wearing out people who don't have your stamina. For example: slow down sometimes, go at the pace of the occasion, don't try and rev it up. Don't give in to every whim, think whether everyone else will want to join in. Ask other people what they would like to do sometimes.

The bonus of being with this kind of person is that they are very good company, have lots of ideas about what to do and where to go and will put energy into making things fun for everyone.

## What can you do if . . .

1. You're shy, like one-to-one situations, loathe big social occasions but have to show up, or on the other hand

2. You love social occasions, particularly parties, but you know you'll probably go mildly manic, get very drunk or behave in such a way that you'll get talked about?

Draw up your own kind of checklist before leaving home. It's more powerful to go into social situations with a positive mental attitude; have your strategy ready and be ready to make the right impression.

## More SSS

✓ I will introduce myself to one or two people if I find myself on my own.

✓ I will prepare one or two topics from this week's news or a current TV show to talk about or ask other people about, then I can listen to them.

✓ If I feel awkward or insecure I won't shrink into my shell, I will give myself a time limit and leave.

✓ If I am likely to show off, I will tell myself to calm down, sit down and get involved in listening not talking.

✓ I am going to wear something that I like, that I feel comfortable in, but I'm going to get an honest friend to check it out in case it's weird.

✓ I'm going to be clear about the image I want to project and either fit in or stand out and be pleased about it.

✓ If I want to smoke I'm going sort out the rules as soon as I arrive and not just light up.

✓ I'm going to weigh up the situation beforehand and decide whether its OK to get drunk.

## Answers

1. A guideline on introductions is that the person who is on home territory or the person who initiated the meeting makes the introductions.

2. (b) Ten minutes allows you to check the arrangements, including how you will settle the bill, before your guest arrives.

3. Don't grovel. A simple apology face to face as soon as possible is the best thing or a short note of apology marked 'Confidential'. If you've ruined someone's jacket, send them flowers.

4. (c) is expedient

(d) might be a wise longer-term solution if you can't stand it.